*Journey with Music*

# Journey with Music

POEMS BY

FRANCIS MAGUIRE

NEW YORK

THE MONASTINE PRESS

Some of these poems have appeared in *Spirit, America, The Sign, Tomorrow, Prairie Schooner* and *The Poetry Chap-Book*. Acknowledgment is made to these publications as well as to D. C. Heath & Company and E. P. Dutton & Company for permission to reprint a number of poems originally published by them.

*Format by Clifford J. Laube*
*Printed in the United States of America*

# CONTENTS

*The Summer-Holders*

# JOURNEY TO THE SEA

We crossed a bridge whose piles were dark
Where moving tides had made their mark.
The grass grew tall, the air grew tense,
Someone or something seemed to cause
A stir charged with magnificence—
And then quite suddenly there it was:
With gulls that whipped and gulls that cried
And sandpipers running on the rim of the tide.

Returning all too soon from this
Miniature Anabasis,
We missed the tug of wind and wing.
Yet there was a feeling in the air
That that great antiseptic thing,
That salty world, would still be there
To cleanse our hearts, engulf our tears,
Tomorrow or in a thousand years.

# THE FOX

Around the cage, around the cage,
And still around, around you run.
O furry fury eyed with flame,
Am I the unforgiven one?

O inextinguishable fire
Whose every flicker is a cry:
"I am a fox. I was betrayed,"
Did Adam do this or did I?

For when he loosed the great winds
That darkened and upturned our sea,
Did Adam wreck his friends the foxes
As well as us, his progeny?

Or is it I, his new accomplice,
Who wake the hatred in your glances?
O would they soften, sullen runner,
If they encountered, say, St. Francis?

But, saints or sinners, others also,
Touched with kinship, dare address you,
And even I may whisper humbly:
"Hapless brother, may God bless you."

# NIGHT PIECE

There is a curious elegance about the town
When the soft-falling snow illuminates the night.
We walk a stranger-prince's hall, a passing clown
Silent and awed, let in by someone's oversight.

Why do we smile? It answers nothing, gives us no
Solutions, fills no hunger, presently will go
As brief, however lovely. What does the evening do
But spill the flakes of snow on flakes of hushed snow?

There is a pristine elegance. The dignity
Of all created things returns to shops not brown
But ermine, opal streets, the gem-encrusted tree.
Eden's own elegance is sifting on the town.

# WHITE LIE

Under the street lights,
Slow, slow,
Piling on sidewalks,
Now the snow

That falls like an airy
Splintered dream
Or imminent music's
Promised gleam

Coming, consoles
By denying, denying,
Veiling the torment,
Muffling the crying,
The dying . . .

Bringing the walker
Soft surcease,
It builds a personal
World of peace

Whose bounds are small
But ineffably sweet —
The snow around us,
The snow at our feet.

And though it is magic
Mixed with guile,
Still we can marvel,
We still can smile . . .
For a while.

## MARCH SONG

Black be the berry
And bitter the fruit
That prick this palate;
Let arrowroot,

A lime, be my dinner
When trees are bud-flecked.
For who can know Spring
But the hungry-elect?

And who knows Easter
Save one astute
To the wizened berry,
The bitter fruit?

## FAIR MARVEL

Few fairer marvels
Are revealed
Than water moving
Through a field,

Or water shining
In a lake
Darkened in
The wind's wake,

Or, slow with wide
Blue mystery,
Water moving
In a sea.

Strange and clear,
On either hand
Water borders
On our land;

And its familiar
Silver line
Runs through many
A town like mine

Where, though now suspect,
Now enchanted,
But somehow never
Taken for granted,

It moves forever
Strange and clear,
Always godlike,
Often dear.

## THE CHARM

Death has come from this small pond,
And for a day or two
The sun does not seem quite so blond,
The water quite so blue.

But soon, but soon these ripples will
Run with a guileless light.
Once more will treble laughter spill
On shores. And this is right.

For waters have a charm against
The sins themselves commit,
And they have grown experienced
By now in using it.

# HE STILL REMEMBERS

He always remembers somehow a sun like steel
That spilled on granite rocks, the shifting beat
Of waves, the taste of swallowed surf, the feel
Of barnacles on seven-year-old feet.
The ridges left on sand when tides withdrew
Like tactile patterns on his mind are stitched,
And the walk home up Beach Bluff Avenue
In the old grey bathing suit that always itched.

And now, though unfamiliar to the sea
As were the summer people to him then,
He still remembers, and he feels that he
Will some day, some day, live near it again
On terms as harsh and intimate and chill . . .
And so perhaps he will, perhaps he will.

# THE SUMMER-HOLDERS

Sunning themselves on river banks and beaches
Or lying prostrate on the still-warm boulders
That border lakes and mark the sea's reaches,
These days you find the few, the summer-holders,
Who know that late-September suns are mellow
As honey made of goldenrod and dew,
That when the trees that circle it are yellow
A pond is no less water nor less blue.

For there is something in them still unstirred
By all the gallant clangor of the fall,
That sees in every southward-flying bird
And hears in each blown leaf and each wind-call
One word, one warning sibilant and bold,—
This: that winter comes and it is cold.

# LUMINOUS AND GOLDEN

Luminous and golden, there it stood,
The sudden radiance of the little wood,
And in the water, like a bright amen,
The leaves, still yellow, held the sun again.

The world is surely full of finer stuff
Than yellow woods, and yet it was enough
To make me want to sing this song about it,
And afterwards the day seemed dull without it.

# THE SNAKE

Though elegant the line and hue
With which he furnishes a brake,
There seems perversely to accrue
But little honor for the snake.

Yet once his handsome embassy
Unpeopled Eden in a season.
Beauty alone — Madame, you see
My song is not without a reason.

## LATE ON A HEAVY AFTERNOON

Late on a heavy afternoon
You watch the leaves' old rigadoon, —
The reds *bouffant,* the lavender lining,
And over the whole dear party somehow
The oblique sun as always shining.
But, deft observer, you join them now
No longer as bright compatriot.
Nature is innocent. You are not.

Too much has occurred to the world and you
To laugh as before in this derring-do.
The heart still undismayed may leap
At a scattered sun and a birch's glint,
But you, watching a pine bough sweep
Like a branch in a Hiroshige print,
Slowly return to the road again,
Glad to be back in the world of men.

# THE ANIMALS

Who are these gods, they ask,
These golden apes, our brothers,
Who take our flesh and fur, and then,
Finding them insufficient, must
Covet each others'?

Each for himself, we choose
To serve or fight them. But
The end is variously the same:
The cards are stacked, the rules are changed.
We always lose.

Yet they, the furred and fed, —
What do they truly win?
For though their incredible caves are warm,
They can shiver within them as we would in
A sudden storm.

    (And so, beholding us,
    The animals discourse,
    And watch us with that wondering look
    At which the pharaohs must have frowned,
    And stare us underground.)

*And Scratching at the Door*

# THE BULL

Beauty is gull,
And goodness hind;
But truth is a bull
Gone wild in the mind.

He tramples the corn,
The fruit, the flowers.
His eyes burn
As your heart cowers.

He murders your swan,
Your goat, your tup —
But woe to the man
Who shuts him up.

# THE RED MOUNTAIN

I saw the red mountain
Bright in the sun.
I turned on my heels
And started to run.

I passed its seekers,
The daring blind.
Faithful bloodhound,
It follows my mind.

Now I am a member
Of mild events,
Never given
To bloody ascents,

Yet there was the mountain,
Sheer rock and height;
And oh, how the summit
Was bright, was bright.

# THE SIN: A DEFINITION

I saw a terrible river
Sweep from eternal space:—
Birds, the sweet trees,
Men, hills, the face
Of firmament, stars
Tumbling, and row on row
Rolled constellations
In tempest-flow.
Suns, saints and even
My body rushed by,
Awful, silent.
And further, I
Sensed in the vision
That what seemed so
Vast merely imaged
A Fearfuller Flow.

I saw a small figure
I knew for my soul
Peer at the river,
Measure the roll,
Step importantly
Into the flood
And walk against it.

Marvel: no blood;
But the river parted
For a soul that said
"I give no glory.
No glory," it said.
O the flow was full
Of earth and sky
And thick with archangels
Floating by.
But against it traveled
A little head.
"I give no glory.
No glory," it said.

# AND SCRATCHING AT THE DOOR

Oh, what poor mangy beast has been
So sinned against as This
Who hears the shut door bolted in
Ungracious emphasis,

Who, hurt and lonely in the wind,
Through the cold night straying,
Hears old familiar tables dinned
And loud music playing,

While we inside still strut or simper,
Sure, as we've been before,
Tomorrow brings a longed-for whimper
And scratching at the door.

# HELP THEM, HEAVEN

Help them, Heaven, who have seen
How delicate a thing is hope —
How slender is the space between
A crowing cock, a whanging rope.

# THE CRAB TREE

The crab tree stands on a bitter plot.
Gnarled and shrunken, it is not
Beautiful. It grows all root.
But I have tasted other fruit.

Another fruit tree I have seen,
All slimness, oh, all starlight sheen.
The crab has roots in a stony well,
But the tree of knowledge grows from hell.

So now to teach these gullible eyes
And minister to this soul, I rise
By frigid morning light to see
This ugly crab, my honest tree.

# AS ONE WHO LEFT A FRAGRANT LAND

As one who left a fragrant land
To climb the dark roads of the sea,
Returning finds his village bland
With patterned sun and leafy tree,

So, Sir, returning to Your isle,
I see again as if anew
Your gentlefolk, how soft their smile;
The grass, how cool; how crisp the dew.

# THE ROOT

The fish are folded
In green seas;
Earth encircles
The shining trees;

Ivy clutches
With multiple art —
But God is a root
Around the heart.

Secret and silent,
He coils around,
Consuming the things
Of the dark ground.

He finds a fissure
Through which to crawl,
Or circles, circles
A tragic wall.

## LET US HONOR HIM SUBTLY, SUBTLY

Let us honor Him subtly, subtly,
As music arches, as bird-songs rain,
Seeking the seeds of glory hidden
Deep in the dignity of the brain.

And if the heart has many windings,
Come, let us thread its devious ways,
Dropping the seeds in secret places
To rise as flowering fields of praise.

Sound as a cherry, deep as an orange —
Gold through from the lustrous rind —
Let us honor Him simply, simply,
With a full heart and a whole mind.

*For the Scarlet Woman*

## THE CITY

Nevertheless don't think for a minute
There is no city. There is, and in it

Is mountain sunlight. And travelers galore,
Believe me, have found it. Now one thing more:

Sometimes a man can judge a town
Better by a stranger who has settled down

There rather than by a native who
Is apt to be blind to the park, the view

From the river, etc., and to have his eyes on
Few things goldener than the horizon.

# THE INCENSE TREE

In the middle of the forest,
Of all sturdy things the fairest,
Of all growing things the dearest,
Stands the radiant incense tree.
Traveler, the trees are falling,
Axes echo in the dwelling,
Winds are rising, hearts are failing.
Where can this poor pilgrim flee?

There the river drowns the rover,
There the lever starves the lover,
There the overseer is ever
Cracking fraying whips in fear.
Are there lips to kiss the crying,
Answers for the sad and sighing,
Songs to fill the futile haying, —
Things for us, the asking, here?

Traveler, recall the story
Of the tree all light and glory,
For it is fact indeed, no faery
Of a far Cathay or Ind.
Beneath it children play, and over
You can see a white bird hover,
And it sends a gentle savor
On the wide, wide wind.

# SONG FOR THE SCARLET WOMAN

If, then, this scented jade, this scarlet woman,
Is truly the beloved of my Lord,
His choice of brides was strange and all-too-human,
His lady scarcely worth such high award,
Unless — unless, perhaps, like some great fountain
That splits the twilight of a jungle wood,
Her honor rises to a bubbling mountain,
Though ringed by darkness, feared, ill-understood.

Oh, scarlet woman, mother, who has words
To show thy glory as a sky of thunder,
Thy sweetness as a branch of singing birds?
With thee are food and drink, and whether under
New England rafters or St. Peter's dome,
Where thou art, lady, there our hearts are home.

# YET ERRING

Yet erring, erring, proud, and lovable,
This upstart, baseborn consort of the King,
Who, should she so desire, could not annul
The timeless terms of His strange marrying.
Her He selected, and her head is high;
In His name speaking, she speaks chaste and true,
Although at times her robes may set awry,
Though they be muddied by her retinue.

Imperfect mother, still a slow beginner
In knowing children and in loving men,
Embarrassed by her saints, like us a sinner,
She falls, and weeps, to fall and rise again,
Until, we pray, that final day will find her
Safe with her Spouse, and us tagging behind her.

*As Flowers*

## MARY NOW

Hard by the plowshare,
Deep in the prairie,
Let us honestly
Honor Mary,
Recalling that native
To this warm earth
Is she, the Chosen,
The Wonder-Birth.

Or soft in the subway,
Let her name
Be a starry window,
A budding flame.
Renew the heart
With the thought that she
Mothers Manhattan
As Galilee.

And, *Tenderest lady,*
Let us say,
*Planes and planets*
*Fly today.*

*Oh, be to one*
*As to the other*
*The gracious queen,*
*The anxious mother.*

*Our bridges bravely*
*Climb on high,*
*But none like you*
*Has spanned the sky.*
*Oh, girl transforming*
*God below,*
*You are our Princess*
*Of Dynamo.*

And she, the lady
Never known blind
To a lover's gesture,
Will be most kind;
And she, the mother,
Will pour release,
Gentle wisdom
And fragrant peace.

# AND REST IN A FLAME

How shall we answer?
What skill, what art
Can cool to reason
This flaming heart

When all of our logic
And all our words
Are a clock's dull ticking,
The cry of birds?

What can we do
But pray, but pray?
That only. And if
It is true, as we say,

That the heart has its logic,
Then it must lead,
How rough the highway,
How slow the speed,

To the town where desire
And reason, the same,
Shall blaze in a Silence
And rest in a Flame.

# NEW ENGLAND LETTER

I tell you this: you grew on earth
That grew on Mather dust,
And Mather ghosts will go with you
Demanding *"Just? . . . Just? . . ."*

I say your bones will ever know
A mountain's white cravasse,
A watcher dark in Wicklow snow
And a young priest saying Mass.

So sin in scarlet as you will,
And laugh as you chase the sun,
But two long winds will whistle through
The dancing skeleton.

# EPITAPH

Sheltered from summer's brazen mirth,
Here by this slender-flowing brook,
There lies a man who since his birth
Lived so aerially it took
Death to bring him down to earth.

# GOOD NIGHT, STRANGER

Coiled and curled
In its secret zones,
Mystery dwells
Beneath your bones,

For warm and alight
With a hidden glow
Is the delicate center
I do not know

Of evils survived
And loves elected.
Yet this is your being
And I respect it.

So now as the casual
Evening ends,
We part, not intimate,
Still good friends;

And though meddling with masks
Is a fool's own danger,
Good night, dear friend, —
And good night, dear stranger.

## ADOLESCENT

He caught his breath today to find
That what was loudest in his mind
Was but the sound upon their ears
Of distant surf on distant piers.

So now his talk is circumspect,
And they are shrewd who can detect
The sick aloneness that imbues
His *Lovely day's* and *How-do-you-do's.*

## QUAINT RIDER

Though quaint indeed your riding habit —
Veil of midnight, frosty guimpe —
Still, madam, you outrun the rabbit,
Outshine the lamp.

For we, no longer to be fooled
By modest hands and downcast eyes,
Know that your way, the hardy-schooled,
Traverses skies.

And even now as here we meet you,
Demurest lady, wherever you are
There on your ride to heaven we greet you —
Girl on a star!

# OH, NO, NOT INDESTRUCTIBLE

Oh, no, not indestructible,
That lovely flowering, the mind.
Weeds grow rampant, florets dull,
And in vain tears we seek to find

The precise borders of cool grass
Where barefoot once we used to run.
The rich black earth like tarnished brass
Pales in the bleaching of the sun,

For many of the springs have dried
And all the rivulets run slow.
The moss and violets have died,
Slow and thin the waters go,

Slow and tragic . . . Still there are
Survivals, — few, perhaps, but fair:
A flower sudden as a star,
A scent like laughter on the air,

As if, for all its poverty,
The garden whispered now and then
The Eden that it used to be,
The glory it will be again.

# PEOPLE AS FLOWERS

If for a moment only, and then ineptly,
Let us consider the people we chance to encounter
As neither lovers nor rivals. Let us consider
People as flowers,
Rare and bud-like, each with his proper fragrance,
Each with a pattern, a hue unshared by the others.
The daisies we know of course, and then the blossoms
Of darksome powers.

But in between are the thousands of thousands of
     species,
The men as well as the women, the stem and stamen
Of body, surely, but also the succulent, tender
Poise of the mind,
And the spirit too, the scented not sighted. But truly
It is not these but the whole, the integral being
That makes the flower. And those who cannot perceive
     it . . .
Are they not blind?

# QUIXOTE

Never believe I do not dread
The merriment in their eyes, he said.
And I laugh too when I think of me
Riding in rusty panoply
On a charger's clumsy counterfeit.
Oh, I'm a very perfect knight.
My armored knees beat a shrill duet,
Each bone beneath is a castanet;
And when my personal music goes
Into the woodland, only the crows
Retain the residential tree.
I know all that, but it sems to me
A man in a lovely lady's thrall
Doesn't mind these things at all,
And to add to her glory a molecule
He'll be a monumental fool.

Now there lived in my neighborhood,
He said, three ladies. One was good;
She loved the poor and the not-quite-bright.
A wiser fool would have been her knight.
Another's wisdom weighted ships
With pilgrims to her narrow lips.
But the third, my lady, is as fair

As any creature anywhere.
Oh, she does not employ her bosom
To pillow a law or a syllogism;
Molded of magic and precision,
Hers is the bare ideal of vision.
She walks for most men under the moon.
She walks by daylight, but only the moon
Transmits her radiance to our clay.
A hero alone can see her by day.

So what does it matter? he concluded.
I'm poor, unworthy, dull, deluded, —
A jest when glasses get unsteady —
But still I serve a beautiful lady.

# REUNION

The hand clasped, the years mellowed
To afternoons in the sun once more.
The old jokes, the antics yellowed
All too soon with a conscious lore.

The honest warmth, but the voice is nearer:
"So the splendid clock ticks a humdrum year."
Then home on the subway, a glance in the mirror,
And fear.

# FABLE

Awakening at night he found
The earth he knew was strangely bound
For somewhere deep and dark in time.
And so he clutched his narrow bed
Against the planetary climb
As winds went wheeling round his head
And years sped by like flying herds
With cries half bovine and half birds'.

Eventually he was able
To call this a fantastic fable,
For though the winds of time be shrill,
Since time and space are in accord,
He had no need to fear; he still
Was in the bosom of the Lord.
And yet it took both prayer and rum
To reach his equilibrium.

# PORTRAIT

No matter how much he drank, his sense of smell was
    sharp.
On his way home that night his nose would not gain-
    say,
Under the honeysuckle, over the lilied water,
The smell of timbers, heavy and imminent with decay.

His eye, a gentleman, saw only gleaming columns,
His ear heard waltzes, gusty laughter, songs of war.
But his nose, barbarian, indelicate reporter,
Found music crumbling softly, and sent him on to
    the bar.

# MEPHISTOPHELES IN THE MORNING

Mephistopheles in the morning finds
Light at an angle which reminds
Him of the farm he lived on before
He had to play these one-night stands
In Cairo, Leeds and Baltimore.
Dew on the grass and mist on ponds
Stir him to neither grief nor fury.
He'd rather feel he's ordinary.

Who wants to concentrate on hell
When the sun rings like an orange bell?
And though sin, perhaps, is a tested tonic,
When birds sound busy as malt in brew
It's hard to be endlessly demonic.
But still if he must . . . he says. And so,
Donning his frayed professional smirk,
He hitches his belt and goes to work.

# NEW ENGLANDER IN THE TROPICS

Amazed by purple seas
And fish with painted bellies,
Outrageous-flowered trees,
Islands of floating lilies,

He gropes his way in the sun,
Hungry for hue and prospect,
Though he shows by an eager frown
Such fruitfulness is suspect.

Where buds like Roman candles
Explode in patterned light
And small quiescent bundles
Erupt in vermilion flight,

Lost in the greens and ochres,
He keeps his stubborn dream
Of a house on neutral acres
By a cold stream.

# THE ILLUMINATED FOUNTAIN

We have come raw from the sea
And climbed cold from the mountain, —
And gladly. We have known
The illuminated fountain

And keep soft-splashing
And misting on the mind
How the drops fall golden
When words fall kind.

Hark to the fragrant laughter
That makes the water blue,
The dream that surges purple,
The love that turns it to

Leaping streams that mirror
A heart's clear glow.
God is good that talking
Is gay and sweet and slow,

And we who have seen it dancing
And watched its jeweled falls
Cascading in reflection
Down clean bare walls

Can face our lonely journey
Back home to sea or mountain
With music. We have known
The illuminated fountain.

*No Sorrow Due*

# YES, DAWN WILL COME

Yes, dawn will come in purple pomp,
And night will go.
The sun will rise all cherry-plump.
I know.

I'll bathe my heart and hands in morning —
Dew-delight.
I know where waters will be turning
Dulcet-white.

But now is night.

# ON THE DROPPING OF A GUISE

Warm and snug about the throat,
It made a handsome overcoat.
No one wore it yet but gained
A cool guise, and self-contained.
But now my coat is wearing thin.
The observant may detect the skin.

Oh, well, a moulting snake forgets
To send his former suit regrets,
And Siegfried thought no sorrow due
The tutor-dwarf he grandly slew.
I too am satisfied.
My guise was useful, but it died.

It's strange how you disdain the buffer
That saved it when the skin gets tougher.
Parents are the bane of hoarse
Adolescent kids of course.
So with my guise. But there is due
At least a decent word or two.

## OLD BONES' TALE

Oh, death will find and maybe fool you,
So cease, man, this crying
For polished bones and fragrant earth
And the clean dispatch of dying.

For, being no more final than
A buried root or bean,
Death, though it may pick your bones,
Will never pick them clean

Of droll, prophetic tales of the
Disgruntled citizen
Who yearned to quit them, yet who will
Inhabit them again.

# ADDRESS TO THE BODY

Body, if age or uppish soul
Should ever cast you down,
Know that I once was warm at home
In this my bony town.

I like my flesh. I like the singing
Girders of the bone.
I like a finger's hinges moving
Silently, alone.

I stand and reverence the heart,
The blood's long train,
The zooming of sensations flying
Up toward the brain.

Body breathing, there are times
One scarce prefers the day
When glory filters out the flesh,
Electrifies the clay.

*Terra Firma*

# THE THIRD WORLD

The third world is music;
Its chemistry: sound.
Evoked from this chaos,
It turns around

In the mind's half-instant,
With seas running fresh
And forests of lyric
But vibrant flesh.

Earth-built and earth-bordered,
Tropics to pole,
This still is the planet
The nostalgic soul

Runs to inhabit,
Tries vainly to hold,
As it spins into darkness
And the night turns cold.

# NOAH'S ARK

Robin and rat both share this house,
Weasel and wolf and lark.
Here is a gull and there a goose,
Sound asleep in the dark.
*Poetry makes strange bedfellows —*
*It builds a Noah's Ark.*

The monkey walks with dignity,
And over his head are stars.
In bright procession rides the snake,
Like a train of emerald cars.
*Poetry song by song can make*
*A zoo that has no bars.*

*So welcome, dove and darkling crow,*
*Proud each of his feather.*
*Lie down, lion, and rest, lamb,*
*Safe here from the weather.*
*Muskrat, elephant, wildcat, doe —*
*Lovely and free together.*

# TERRA FIRMA

Can it be then that this, this airy platform
Alone is *terra firma* to the feet
That left the level roadway seeking something
High and sweet? —

But for a moment only, or for a day.
For from the choicest tower, the noblest steeple,
A man remembers frogs and flowers, and he
Remembers people.

And if he climbs too often or too long,
Descending he will find the street a Babel.
To live there as before he is not willing
And not quite able.

# THE GIRL WITH HER HAIR IN A
## GOLDEN SNOOD

"The girl with her hair in a golden snood
Didn't wind up in Hollywood;
Our genius, chastened, farms his glen —
So who are you, man, to bother us?
Limberer lads and wiser men
Than you have died anonymous,
And if you're snug in the grace of God
What if you rest in a nameless sod?"

True, and *negator caveat*,
But for some it's not as easy as that.
Unsainted, futile, we still would stay
The dusk of time with some poor clue,
A word, an empire, a tomb, to say:
"Here was a man who lived like you,
Learned a little and wondered much.
He died, and his name was Such-and-such."

*Indigo World*

# THE WORMS

A man of wisdom is on terms
Of friendship with whatever squirms
Beneath the earth — for instance worms.

For they remember. Circled in
Their seven hells they yearn to spin
Their tunnels through the scented skin
Of those who use their kith and kin

As silken slaves, perhaps, or bait.
Ah, shudder, friend, and contemplate
The vengeances these men await,
Their shock when they must face the fate

Of yielding all their mortal worth
To these poor instruments of mirth,
The meek inheritors of earth.

# HOUSE ON SAND

It's not a pretty thing
To see a house humbled, —
To see your house and land
All, all tumbled
By rain, wind, torrent,
And broken by the sea.
It's hard to walk a sand dune
Bare of turf or tree
And know it was a garden
Where once you used to lie on
A warm autumn evening
And watch proud Orion
Glimmering like spear-heads
Full of far disasters,
Falling like a white cloud,
Cool among the asters.

It's hard, I say, and therefore
If we seem slow
In building up again
Our homes and gardens, know
It's a brief page in history,
Though long by the clock,
To search about the landscape

And dig down to rock
To build a strong cellar
With surety behind it.
For once we had a promise
That there we should find it.

# NOTE FROM THE CONTINENT

It is as we expected. The sunlit cathedrals
We knew have been sunken, engulfed by the waves of
    our time,
And now and then only, and muffled by steeples of
    water,
Bells chime.

It is as they had told us. The three-noted singers
That splintered our dawns have returned. Though they
    improvise,
It is hardly singing. They scratch but an interruption
On somber skies.

It is as we had feared it. The heart, dark-wounded
From following hard on the heels of an ingrate mind,
Now moves slowly and limps among the townsmen
It left behind.

We knew and we feared this; and yet, though un-
    uttered,
This too we knew and now it is witnessed by time:
That a heart can stir always (though slowly), that
    birds sing (somewhere)
And bells chime.

[ 84 ]

# SWEET LAND

In loving you, sweet land, we love a thing
Dearer than any acre dreamed of now.
Oh, some of us are sick for hills in spring,
And others yearn for fields they used to plow;
But, knowing these, we knew an atmosphere
Of sunlight streaming through a blossoming tree,
Of winds between the oceans, vast and clear,
That sang: sweet land, sweet land of liberty.

For what they sang is your excuse for being,
The element, my land, in which you live.
It is a climate found but ever fleeing,
A fragrant empire love nor lease can give
But subjects everywhere may serve and share.
And look: the world around us! Sniff the air!

# A DIRTY WORLD, AND MINE

## I.

The things that happened happened in my day.
I saw the artificial jungle grow.
Potassium nitrate added to a lie,
Chemical feeding of the seed you sow —
And there, thick as the upper Amazon
With creepers, lianas round a rotting tree,
There was the jungle in this our temperate zone,
And underneath it, stumbling, there were we.

The night the ants attacked, our comrades' screams
Were drowned in the chattering of monkeys. We
Felt dreadful, dreadful, but hardly enough, it seems.
At the moment in a clearing, we'd surely be
Fools if . . . Still it gave us quite a turn.
We had so much, we had so much to learn.

## II.

But why should a man stand at his own front door,
Press the lipstick on a trembling mouth
And then embark for some outlandish shore, —
The S. S. Malaria, maybe, heading south?
No ship that takes its weather from the *Times,*
Whose beacons are commercial radio towers,

Will carry us, we said. So we made rhymes
Of reason, went to the movies, bought some flowers.

The wind that traveled meanwhile past the house
Was history enormous on the run.
Now we could feel it — it was getting close —
See how its dust was darkening the sun,
Even admire it, standing yet aloof, —
Until the night it tore away the roof.

### III.

No, there is no escape. No Shangri-la,
No Arden now awaits the refugee.
No Attic lamb emits a pastoral baa;
Atlantis, if it is, is in the sea.
Nor can I look in my own heart and say
"Christ's kingdom, ringed with peace, at least is here."
No. His treaties too we let decay.
The world and I both settled for small beer.

Whatever the world is, I belong to it.
Call it a picnic grounds alive with the shine
Of broken bottles, comics, cans of Flit,
It is a dirty world, and it is mine.
But mine too is the other, slowly growing,
Where winds are new and a warm rain is blowing.

# MAIDANEK

"I found this teddy bear in the warehouse, too.
I picked it up from a pile of similar dolls,
mostly rag or cloth like this, but a few
of china . . ." Unquote. *PM*. And so the walls
of Maidanek synthesize a people's cries
into one word, and here is the word they speak:
a teddy bear (photographed in actual size)
no longer warm against a frightened cheek.

And when the loudspeakers played that waltz of Strauss
to drown the sounds in the Trempitsky forest,
then where were you, my soul, in what warm house,
how deep in work or prayer? Oh, God, the fairest
agendum in this age so great with wrong
is to put small teddy bears back where they belong.

## BE SILLY, GIRLS

Be silly, girls. Explode in giggles,
Splatter the bus with snorts and squeals.
Fit as fiddles and rude as beagles,
And just as sedate as a pair of eels,
You're loud, you know. And *where* were you taught
To look that way at a sailor — to move
Your lids, then collapse in snickers? You're not
Being ladies. Your teachers would disapprove.

Yet still be silly. The boy has heard
Small teen-age snickering this year.
And yours he keeps as a coin, a word
Preserved for the others, the schooled-in-fear —
Rebecca, Masha, Morning Dew —
Who should be giggling girls with you.

# INDIGO WORLD

So open now the door,
The stare may melt.
The things but seen before
May now be felt.

The frigid, accurate eye
Served watcher, sleeper.
But perspicacity
Must now go deeper,

And tear ducts, knotted, gnarled,
At last may flow
Over a winter world
Grown indigo.

# NO GENTLE WORD

So through those years and through the self-same
 torrent
Another and another man has passed.
Then who am I to hold it as abhorrent
That mellowing begins its work so fast? —
That, entertaining friends around a fire,
They find their tales in telling turn to gold,
Though on one path their comrades choked in mire
And on another others died of cold?

But these were fearful things! We must not have
Some kindly eye deny the truth it saw.
The men who died no gentle word will save,
And cheap remembrance robs us of the awe
That should enkindle every heart alive
Who knows what men can meet with — and survive.

*The Fact*

# IT'S STILL HOSANNAH

Other men, my pharisee,
Your bright hosannahs may deceive.
Strangers you may fool, perhaps,
But never, never, never me.

That quisling heart, how often it
Has proved a traitor to your words
I know, remember. If I were you,
I'd keep my mouth shut, hypocrite.

*Yet will I praise the Lord.* There be
Two things a son like me may sing:
The first of these is God the Fact,
The other His mercy as the sea.

So, sure of the one, for the other bolder,
*Mercy,* I'll sing, and *Glory, glory.*
Yes, though the devil stand and slip
A familiar arm around my shoulder.